2S0

SOMETHING ABIDES

The Story
of
Joshua Chamberlain

by
John J. Pullen

ISBN 0-9704408-1-2

Cover Design by Mason Philip Smith

Cover illustration "Hold At All Costs"
courtesy of Dale Gallon Historical Art
Gettysburg, PA www.gallon.com

Back cover photo courtesy of Renee Chevalier
Book layout by Patricia Hodgdon

Printed and bound in the United States of America

Published by 20th Maine, Inc.
49 West Street, Freeport, ME 04032
(207) 865-4340
www.20thmaine.com

For

Philip

Acknowledgements

The creation and production of this book truly is a “labor of love“...love and respect, that is. It started with the respect and reverence that one man, John J. Pullen, modern-day author and historian, had for another, Joshua L. Chamberlain, 19th century professor, soldier, and statesman. Having studied Chamberlain’s life for a good deal of his own, John Pullen recognized the great value in telling young people the story of a life of integrity, duty and honor.

The publication of this book results from the collaborative efforts of many who admired, respected and loved John Pullen. Like Chamberlain, John Pullen’s life is an example that we can aspire to. Out of friendship and gratitude for all that he gave to others, the following people freely offered their assistance in bringing this, his last book, to print.

If John was writing his own acknowledgements, he surely would thank his wife, Margaret. Her devotion and constant care during his illness enabled him to finish his life doing what he loved best — writing.

To say that this publication would not have been possible without the work of Rita Bailey is an understatement. Rita served tirelessly as John’s editorial assistant, research assistant, editor, friend and a champion of his work. Rita is a remarkable woman who is almost as much a part of this book as John.

Margaret Pullen and the publisher also wish to thank Sarah Thomas of Thomas Publications for an extensive, professional editing job and other assistance. Thank you also to William and Ellen Marvel who edited the early manuscripts and the glossary, Sean Crean, Judy McAfee and Amanda Cover for their very valuable suggestions on the text.

Three young men, Brendan and Ryan Keating and Aubrey Cover read the manuscript and gave important input from the age group targeted by the book.

The following people and organizations freely provided the photos that compliment the text and thereby make the whole production more interesting to young readers:

- Bedford & Janet Hayes, Gunsight Antiques
- Pejepscot Historical Society, Brunswick, ME
- Gallon Historical Art, Gettysburg, PA
- Renee Chevalier
- Peter Moulton

To Our Young Readers

There is a lot of stuff in this book you may not understand at first. For example, words about war. We hope you never will have any experience of that. The war you will be reading about is the American Civil War. It happened so long ago that few people know much about it now. And many words that everyone knew then need explanation now. We have marked these words with this symbol. * When you see one of these and you don't understand the word, please turn to the GLOSSARY at the back of the book.

John

Table of Contents

		Page
Introduction		8
Chapter 1	The Early Years	13
Chapter 2	A Path to Glory	18
Chapter 3	The Road to Little Round Top	26
Chapter 4	Grant Takes Over the Army	38
Chapter 5	Honor Answering Honor	46
Chapter 6	Civilian Life Again	49
Chapter 7	The Final Years	54
Glimpses of the Old General		58
Glossary		60

Introduction

A Good Read

This is Dixie! She belongs to Patricia and Ron and they belong to her. The book she is holding was written a long time ago by John J. Pullen; it was published in 1957. Its hero is Joshua Chamberlain.

Introduction

Patricia and her husband Ron have sold many books about Joshua Chamberlain for adults in their shop in Freeport, Maine. "But" Patricia said, "we ought to have one for younger readers."

Patricia began to write the special book for youngsters, but the shop was keeping her too busy. So she asked John Pullen, the author of ***The Twentieth Maine*** to do it. He wrote a number of pages but was not satisfied with them. "I've never written anything for young people," he said: "I can't quite seem to get the hang of it."

Introduction

John has a grandson named Philip and Philip has a father named Mark who writes for journals. John showed Mark the pages he had written. Reading these pages with Philip, Mark then made some suggestions that would make the story more understandable even to children.

John also wanted to recheck some of the facts about Joshua Chamberlain's life to make sure as possible that he told the true story. He called upon his friend Rita who has had much experience in Civil War research. Here she is reading letters and documents in the Special Collections Department of the Bowdoin College library. John also asked boys and girls and their teachers to read his manuscript and their comments were most helpful. To help with words that may be hard to understand, he added a "Glossary" to the back of the book.

In the meantime, John was serving on a committee planning to put up a statue of Joshua Chamberlain in Brunswick, Maine. In December of 2000 the committee was interviewing a number of sculptors who wanted to create this statue. The turn of sculptor Joseph Query came and he entered the room carrying a ragged, paperback copy of ***The Twentieth Maine.*** He said he had found the book in Naples, Italy when he was a student there in 1963 and was looking around for something written in English to read. He saw ***The Twentieth Maine***! He read it over and over and became deeply interested in Joshua Chamberlain. The committee chose Joseph Query unanimously, not just because of his interest in Joshua Chamberlain, but also the high quality of his work and excellent reputation in the field of sculpture.

Here is Joseph Query in his studio sculpting the statue.

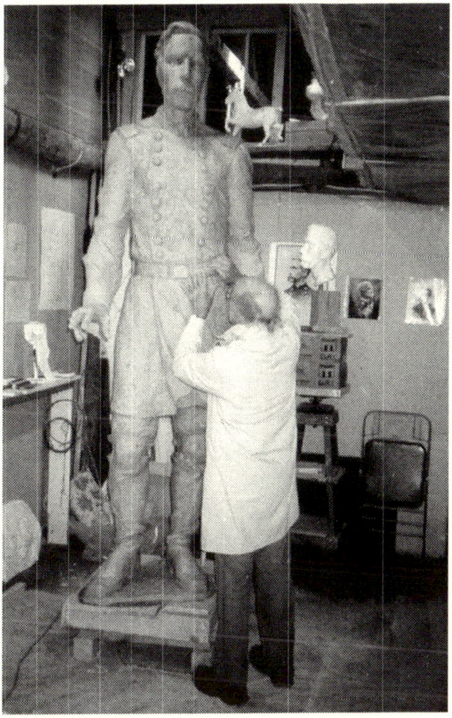

Introduction

Here is the finished statue of Joshua Chamberlain by sculptor Joseph Query in a foundry where, with a process used for centuries, a figure created in clay and cast into plaster is finally transformed into bronze.

And this is the story of…….

Joshua Chamberlain

Image Courtesy of Bedford Hayes

The Early Years

Statue of Joshua Chamberlain
Brunswick, Maine
Photo by Ron Hodgdon

In the spring of the year 2002 Sculptor Joseph Query completed a statue of General Joshua Chamberlain, Maine's greatest soldier and one of its greatest citizens. It stands in Brunswick, Maine, in front of the building that was once his home. This is the story of Joshua Chamberlain's life.

He was born on September 8, 1828 in Brewer Maine, to Joshua and Sarah Chamberlain. Brewer is on the great Penobscot River, just across the river from the City of Bangor. His parents were farmers. Their farm was not far from the big forest that covers most of northern Maine.

He was named Lawrence Joshua Chamberlain. The "Lawrence" came from Captain* James Lawrence, an officer of the U. S. Navy. Captain Lawrence was wounded in a sea battle. As he lay dying he shouted to his men "Don't give up the ship." It was a good name for the new baby, for he grew up to be a man who would never give up.

For some reason Chamberlain did not like the name the way it was. He switched it from Lawrence Joshua Chamberlain to Joshua Lawrence Chamberlain. He had three brothers, Horace, John and Tom and a sister, Sarah, whom he always called "Sae." They kept right on calling him Lawrence. But almost everybody else called him Joshua, as we do.

The Early Years

Growing up on a farm meant doing lots of hard work - chopping, sawing and splitting wood, mowing and pitching hay, hoeing, clearing rocks from the fields and other exercises. Joshua built up a strong body. He learned to ride horses and sail on the river. One summer day Joshua was

Haying in the 19th Century. Image courtesy of Bedford Hayes

pitching hay and loading it onto a wagon. A wheel of the wagon got caught between two stumps. Getting it free seemed impossible. His father was working nearby. "How am I going to do it?" Joshua called to his father. "Do it, that's how!" his father shouted. Joshua grabbed the hub of the wheel. He gave a mighty heave. The oxen pulled and the hay wagon came out. Always afterwards Joshua remembered "Do it, that's how!" when he had something hard to do.

He attended the local school and was a very good student. He learned music and became an excellent singer. He obtained a bass viol, but there was no bow for it so he made one out of a corn stalk. His musical talent would be important to him later in life. Often his father went into the great forests to the North to survey timberlands and sometimes Joshua went with him. He enjoyed seeing moose, bears and other animals, but there is no record that he ever hunted or trapped them.

Joshua climbed Mt. Katahdin, Maine's highest mountain. He met native Americans and learned about their language, customs and crafts.

Like all youngsters, Joshua wondered what he was going to do when he grew up. His father wanted him to go to the U.S. Military Academy at West Point and become an army officer. His mother wanted him to become a minister in the church. He decided to follow her advice and go to Bowdoin College to prepare for the ministry. There were academic requirements for entrance to Bowdoin including Latin and Greek. He set up a rigorous schedule for himself; first, setting up a room in his attic for study. Every day at 10:00 a.m. he walked a mile and a quarter to Bangor to the "Chatham University" in a stable-loft in General Stevens barn, across the street from the Bangor Theological Seminary. There he spent 3 hours of instruction and reciting his lessons, then came home to study in his attic retreat. He followed this schedule each day from 5:00 a.m. to 10:00 p.m. until he felt he knew enough of these ancient languages to qualify for Bowdoin.

Image Courtesy of Peter Moulton.

Bowdoin College in Brunswick, Maine opened a whole new world for Joshua. He studied subjects like history, philosophy, mathematics, literature and languages. There was a big church near the campus, the First Parish Church where Joshua attended services. In time he became Director of Music. While directing the choir he met a dark-haired beauty named Fanny Adams, who sometimes played the organ. They fell in love but decided not to marry until Joshua became a minister.

Francis Adams Chamberlain
Courtesy of Pejepscot Historical Society

Joshua graduated from Bowdoin in 1852. Then he went north to study for the ministry at the Bangor Theological Seminary. Fanny went south to Milledgeville, Georgia, where she taught classes in voice and piano. For three years they did not see each other, but kept in touch by letter. At last came the happy day when Joshua came back from Bangor, having graduated from the theological school, and Fanny was back from Georgia. Then something rather unexpected happened.

Bangor Theological Seminary, Bangor, Maine
Image Courtesy of Peter Moulton

Life is sometimes peculiar. We make plans but things do not always turn out the way we expect. Joshua never became a minister. Here's what happened.

Joshua gave a talk at the 1855 Bowdoin College Commencement*. Giving a talk is a good way to get noticed. The trustees and overseers were so impressed that they offered him a job as an instructor and he accepted.

Now Fanny and Joshua could get married because Joshua would be making enough money to support a family. They were married on December 7, 1855, in the First Parish Church were they had first met. They settled into a little home on Potter Street, near the Bowdoin College campus. It was a house where the poet Henry Wadsworth Longfellow had once lived, when he was a professor at Bowdoin. Fanny and Joshua lived there with their two children, Grace and Harold Wyllys.

Image Courtesy of Pejepscot Historical Society

The old Chamberlain residence before being remodeled.
Corner Potter & Maine Streets

While a student Joshua always had trouble with mathematics but he was good at languages. He continued to study until the languages he knew included Latin, Greek, Hebrew, Arabic, Syriac, French, German and Spanish. In 1861 Bowdoin College made him a professor and head of the Department of Modern Languages. It was an important job, and his future looked bright. Better still, it allowed him a leave of two years to study languages in Europe. But then his life took another turn that he had not planned.

A Path to Glory

It was another odd twist of fate that Joshua Chamberlain would gain fame as a soldier, as his father would have wished. This was not even his decision. The political situation in America brought it about. Reading the newspapers, Joshua and Fanny had seen for several months that trouble was brewing. A dark cloud hung over the nation.

At this time some of the people in the Southern states - mostly the big plantation* owners - had slaves. Slaves were people of all ages collected and brought from Africa by slave-traders. The slave-trader would go into a native village, give false promises of a better life or even kidnap the natives to get the number of slaves he needed for his business. He would then take these innocent people to a far-away slave-market where they were bought by anyone who could pay the price. In this cruel system family members were often separated forever. They could be sold to an abusive master, made to live in squalid conditions and always had to work very hard. Since many people were needed to work on the large rice and cotton plantations nearly all of the slave-markets were held in the South. Without slave labor the owners thought they could not supply the cotton and rice needed by America and England.

In 1850 there were 30 states in the Union. Trouble started when new states formed in the Western territories began to be admitted to the Union. The South thought these new states should allow slavery. The North thought all people in the new states should be free.

The South said the Constitution meant for each state to make its own decision on such questions such as to be a slave or free state. This interpretation was called states' rights by the South. But it was disputed by the Federal government.

The South was concerned that if the new states joining the Union were slave-free then, perhaps all of the states would follow. If this happened they would lose all of the money they had spent to buy the slaves as well as lose their needed workers. Some people in the South even threatened to leave the Union and set up another nation if slavery was abolished.

Feelings were running high as the election of 1860 approached. Abraham Lincoln, who was against slavery, was a candidate. He said it this way, "The nation cannot exist half-slave and half-free."

Abraham Lincoln
Image Courtesy of Patricia Hodgdon

When Lincoln was elected in 1860 eleven of the Southern states decided to secede* – to leave the Union, as they threatened to do. They formed another nation, called the Confederate States of America,* or sometimes the Confederacy for short. In one of their states, South Carolina, their soldiers fired cannons on a fort (Fort Sumter) that belonged to the United States, now considered to be another nation, and forced the men inside to surrender. This started the Civil War in the spring of 1861.

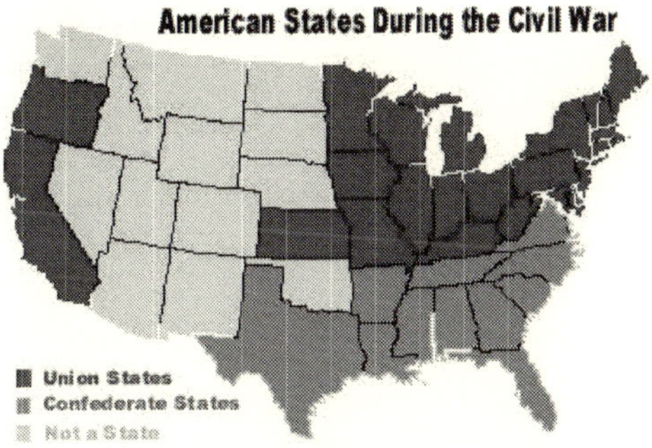

A Path to Glory

Abraham Lincoln called for men to enlist in the Army* and Navy and help save the Union. Thousands volunteered. At Bowdoin College many boys left the classrooms and went off to war. Joshua Chamberlain did not go in 1861 because he had a wife and family to support. Besides, everybody thought the war would be over in a few months because the North was so much bigger and stronger than the South, with more people, more factories, and more of almost everything.

However, the men of the South were very good soldiers. They won the very first battle. This took place around a stream called Bull Run 25 miles southeast of Washington on July 21, 1861. Some people from Washington had gone out to see the battle carrying their picnic baskets. They and the Northern soldiers had to run for their lives. They found that war is no picnic. By the summer of 1862 the war was still not going well at all for the North. Their army, under General McClellan, had tried to capture Richmond, the capital of the Confederacy, but had failed. Then the North had suffered another defeat at Bull Run; Lincoln called for more volunteer regiments to come and put down the rebellion.*

General George McClellan
Image Courtesy of Patricia Hodgdon

At Bowdoin College, Joshua Chamberlain decided he would join one of the new regiments. He was 34 years old. The College did not want him to go. His family did not want him to go. But Joshua was determined that he would help save the United States. He thought "If we don't save it now we will soon have no country to save, I can't stand to see that happen." Joshua applied to the Governor of Maine, who made him lieutenant colonel* of one of the new regiments, the 20th Regiment Infantry, Maine Volunteers. This placed him second in command of the regiment.

We suppose his friends said," Now what are you going to do? You don't know anything about that military stuff." And Joshua could have said "I'll learn."

Colonel Adelbert Ames
Photo Courtesy of Bedford Hayes

The men of the 20th Maine gathered at Camp Mason, near Portland. They were farmers, woodsmen, fishermen, clerks, laborers, teachers – all kinds of people. They were good men, but they knew absolutely nothing about being soldiers. Their commander was Colonel* Adelbert Ames. He knew what war was like. He was a graduate of West Point and had been wounded at the first battle of Bull Run. Colonel Ames was very concerned when he saw his men for the first time. He probably said to Joshua "They will all be killed if we cannot get them trained in time for their first battle." Also they must be disciplined because in battle soldiers get very excited and frightened so they must act from habit - and that habit must be stronger than the fear of death. That's what discipline is.

A Civil War regiment* numbered about 1000 men. They were divided into ten companies,* called Company A, B, C, D, E, F, G, H, I, K. (There was no Company J because "J" could be mistaken for "I" in handwriting.) The regiment was commanded by a colonel. Second in command was a

Tom Chamberlain
Photo Courtesy of Bedford Hayes

lieutenant colonel* (that was Joshua Chamberlain's job). Chamberlain's brother Tom was also in the regiment. He enlisted as a private* and soon became a sergeant.*

How to move and march as a team was one thing the men had to be taught. In moving from one place to another they usually marched in columns of fours.*

Marching, they had to all keep in step and keep closed up in a tight group to take as little space on the road as possible. But in combat they had to spread out in two lines of battle.*

Going from one formation into another (or back again) took a lot of training and practice or else they would be stepping on one another's feet and getting all mixed up.

Soldiers also required training in the use of the musket* or rifle. Civil War weapons were not as easy to load and fire as those of today. Ammunition had to be loaded into the muzzle* of the rifle and rammed down into the barrel with a ramrod. Loading the gun took nine different motions. Unless the soldier did all this by discipline and habit, in his excitement he would make mistakes. He might even forget to remove the ramrod and fire it off into the air - leaving himself unable to load and fire any more.

Lieutenant Colonel Chamberlain and the other new officers had to know all these things before they could teach the soldiers to do them. They learned from books. And Colonel Ames who had learned by experience also taught them. Joshua Chamberlain was a quick learner and most of the other new officers were well educated, so they could study and learn. But there was little time to teach the men before they had to leave their camp in Maine. There were many things to do - like getting uniforms and arms for them and getting organized into companies.

The 20th Maine traveled by railroad and steamboat to Washington, DC. They arrived on Sunday, September 7, 1862. Next day at an arsenal* they received rifles and ammunition. Then they marched to a camp called Fort Craig across a bridge over the Potomac River. On the way they marched very badly. They could not keep in step and they straggled. Bystanders along the way laughed at them. Colonel Ames was disgusted. He yelled, "If you can't do any better than that you all ought to desert and go home." This remark angered the men but made them try harder to show Colonel Ames he was wrong about them.

At Fort Craig the 20th Maine became part of the Army of the Potomac. It was assigned to the Third Brigade* of the First Division* of the Fifth Corps of this Army.

General Robert E. Lee
Image Courtesy of Patricia Hodgdon

Soon news came that the army of the South, called the Army of Northern Virginia, was invading the North. This army was commanded by a great general, Robert E. Lee.

A Path to Glory

Everyone became very alarmed. On September 12, 1862 the Army of the Potomac marched out to stop them. It was commanded by General George McClellan. On the march, it was very hot and dusty. The men of the 20th Maine began to sweat and suffer. Their new shoes made blisters on their feet. They grew thirsty - then weary - then exhausted. Some dropped out. Then more dropped out until finally there were only a few men left at the end of a 17-mile march. It looked as though the regiment had been lost but next morning, to everyone's surprise, the regiment was almost full strength again. The drop-outs had picked themselves up and caught up during the night. On this day the weather was cooler and the 20th Maine marched with the army 24 miles. People along the way were waving flags, giving them water to drink and cheering them on.

They marched through a gap in a mountain range on September. They knew they were approaching the Southern army because they saw that Northern troops marching ahead of them had been fighting. They found trees gashed by bullets and shell fragments, torn-up earth, splintered buildings, and dead soldiers. Joshua saw a Southern soldier sitting upright with his back against a tree. When he went nearer he realized that the soldier was dead and was only 16 or 17 years old. He was holding a little Bible in his hand. It probably had been given to him by his mother, and he must have been clutching it when he died. Chamberlain thought "Is this the enemy?" It was his first look at the awfulness of war.

The next day Joshua and the 20th Maine saw their first battle - fortunately from a distance because their 5th Corps was held back in reserve.* They saw cannon and rifles flashing, clouds of smoke, men falling. They heard the thunder of artillery* shells* and the rattle of musketry.* They saw bloody wounded men walking or being carried from the field. It was the worst slaughter of the Civil War. More than 5000 men were killed in one day. It was the Battle of Antietam, September 17, 1862.

The invasion was halted. General Lee took his army back across the Potomac. The 20th Maine was part of a group that waded across the shallow river and tried to chase them. But a large force of Southerners turned back and counter-attacked. The Northern soldiers were ordered to retreat. Joshua Chamberlain sat on his horse in the middle of the river steadying his men while the bullets rained down from a bluff where the Southerners were firing. His horse was hit. Three men were wounded. This was their first combat experience, but they did not panic.

On October 1 President Lincoln came to visit the army for several days. The whole army lined up for him to review*. Lincoln rode down the line beside General McClellan. When he came opposite the 20th Maine he noticed Joshua Chamberlain's beautiful white horse. He stopped and looked at it. Did he look at Lt. Col. Chamberlain too? Maybe. Anyway, Joshua never forgot this moment.

Abraham Lincoln &
General McClellan at Antietam.
Courtesy of the
Library of Congress

The Road to Little Round Top

October and November 1862 were hard months for the 20th Maine. Colonel Ames put them through the training they needed so badly. He worked the soldiers so hard that they hated him. Tom Chamberlain wrote home that he thought someone would shoot Ames in the back when they got into battle. But after a while when they began to march and maneuver* well, they started to feel proud of themselves. Joshua told them that they would soon be glad that they had this tough training.

At night in their tent, Joshua received special instruction from Colonel Ames. He read military manuals by candle light. He read a book called "The Art of War." He enjoyed the outdoor life. In another letter Tom wrote "You should see Lawrence riding on his white horse and giving commands. He looks great!" But soon the weather turned cold. The government had not provided good food or enough shelter tents. Soldiers began to die of exposure and disease. Doctors of that time did not have the knowledge and the medicines that they have today. In the Civil War sickness killed twice as many men as bullets and shells. Joshua Chamberlain had to attend many burial services. Around three hundred 20th Maine soldiers died of disease during the war. It made him very sad.

General Ambrose Burnside

The Army of the Potomac moved slowly south following the retreat of the Army of Northern Virginia. Too slowly, President Lincoln thought, so he fired its commander, General McClellan. He replaced him with General Burnside, who had a peculiar style of whiskers and was not always very bright. General Burnside put the army into the battle of Fredericksburg.

It was a disaster. The troops had to cross a river and then advance uphill against an enemy firing from behind a stone wall and other entrenchments.* It was the first real battle for the 20th Maine. Colonel Ames and Lt. Col. Chamberlain led the regiment as far as they could go – then they had to lie down behind a slight ridge in the ground, or they would have all been killed. It was mid-December and very cold. They lay there all night among hundreds of wounded who were moaning and crying.

President Lincoln next removed General Burnside as the army commander and replaced him with General Hooker. Hooker did a number of good things. He improved the soldiers' shelter and food. He introduced a system whereby a soldier could look at other soldiers' badges, flags and colors and tell instantly what military unit it was. This prevented much confusion in battles.

General Hooker took the army into the battle of Chancellorsville. The 20th Maine could not go because the men had been vaccinated* to protect them against smallpox. But the vaccine was bad: it did not protect them instead it gave them the smallpox and the 20th Maine was quarantined.* Colonel Ames got himself detached and went to the battle. Chamberlain went to army headquarters and said "Let me take the regiment in - at least we could give the enemy the smallpox!" "Nothing doing," was the answer. The battle was another disaster and defeat for the North.

The Road to Little Round Top

Colonel Ames did very well in the battle of Chancellorsville. On May 20th he was promoted to brigadier general* and given another assignment. This meant that Joshua Chamberlain was now in command of the 20th Maine. He was promoted to Colonel. Mostly because of losses at Fredericksburg and those caused by sickness, the regiment was now down to about 400 men instead of the 1000 it had started with. It needed replacements. The replacements arrived - 120 men from the 2nd Maine. But these men refused to fight. The term of service for the 2nd Maine had ended and the rest of the regiment had gone home. Because of a misunderstanding these men had been kept in service. This was wrong, they thought, so they mutinied.* Orders to Chamberlain were that if they would not serve they should be shot. But Chamberlain talked to them, and all but six did agree to join the 200 and continue to fight. Chamberlain showed real leadership, and you will soon see how important it was.

Early June 1863 found the two armies facing each other across the Rappahannock River in Virginia, watching each other carefully. Soon it was noticed that the Southern soldiers were disappearing. They had slipped away into a valley to the west, and were headed north. Another invasion!* The Southerners were saying "We've whipped the Yankees twice. Now we'll go whip them again up North and end the war!" Seven corps of the Army of the Potomac started North as fast as they could go. They were ordered to stay between General Lee's forces and Washington and bring them to battle somewhere. Colonel Chamberlain led the 20th Maine away from the Rappahannock on June 13. They marched the rest of the month through long, hot, dusty and thirsty days that left the men exhausted at night. Several days they marched 20 miles - on one day, 26! It was a terribly long way to go.

The Road to Little Round Top

On July 1 they marched more than 25 miles. That afternoon they heard the sound of cannon off to the west. When they arrived at Hanover, Pennsylvania, they saw dead soldiers and horses lying around. Northern and Southern cavalry* had fought there.

Colonel Chamberlain had just ordered his men to pitch tents for the night when a messenger came galloping up. He had bad news. Two corps of the Army of the Potomac had run into the Confederate army at a town called Gettysburg, about 17 miles to the west. They had been defeated and driven back through the town. They had taken a position on some high ground east of Gettysburg. They desperately needed the other five corps of the army to come help them.

The Town of Gettysburg at the time of the battle with the Round Tops in the distance.

Brady Photograph

When Lincoln heard that there was going to be a big battle at Gettysburg he became very anxious. He knew that if the South won, the Confederate States would probably be recognized as a separate nation by England and other countries. Then the people of the North would want to negotiate an end to the war. The United States would be broken in two.

Joshua Chamberlain told his men that he knew they were tired - they had already marched 25 miles that day. But their corps, the Fifth Corps, was moving to Gettysburg, so they had to get up and drive on. They marched through the night.

The Road to Little Round Top

The moon was shining. People along the way had heard that their state was being invaded by the Confederates. They were alarmed and excited. They rushed from their homes by the roadside to wave flags and welcome the Union soldiers. Bands played. The people cheered and white handkerchiefs fluttered from the windows. The 20th Maine reached Gettysburg at dawn on July 2, 1863 almost exhausted. The men stretched out on the ground to sleep.

General George Gordon Meade

While the soldiers of the 20th Maine and other men of the Fifth Corps rested, the battlefield was fairly quiet. But troops were getting into position along a line that looked something like a big fishhook. The army was now commanded by General Meade. (General Hooker had been resigned.) The line chosen by General Meade was four or five miles long. Its southern end rested on a rocky little hill called Little Round Top.

Little Round Top (left) & Big Round Top (right).
Brady Photograph

General Meade thought that he had troops on Little Round Top and it was adequately defended. This was not true. There were only a few men up there waving signal flags. This was discovered late in the afternoon when officers went to Little Round Top and found that it was undefended. Even worse a massive Confederate force was approaching from the west. If the Confederates got Little Round Top they would flank* the whole Union line! They could get cannon on top of the hill, fire lengthwise down that line and force the Army of the Potomac to retreat! The word went out: "Get some troops up here as fast as possible!" The Fifth Corps was then drawing near to this part of the battlefield and the brigade the 20th Maine was in was near Little Round Top. When the brigade commander, Colonel Strong Vincent, heard that troops were needed there, he did not even wait for orders. He hustled the brigade off at the double quick* to this important hill.

When the regiment reached the position it was to occupy, there was not much time left. The Confederates were getting close. Chamberlain gave his command, "On the right by file into line!" This called for a rather complicated maneuver, but it took each man out of marching formation and into line of battle ready to fire. The 20th Maine did it perfectly. Their training under Ames and Chamberlain had paid off.

Colonel Vincent told Chamberlain "You are on the very end of the Union line. You are to hold this position at all costs!" Chamberlain knew what that meant. If the 20th Maine gave way, the whole Union line might be flanked. It would be do or die here.

Chamberlain did not put all 10 companies of the 20th Maine into line of battle on Little Round Top. He sent one company, Company B, off into the woods on his left front. In that position they could give him warning if any enemy force came from that direction. The men of Company B disappeared into the trees. We will find out later what happened to them.

The hill that the 20th Maine occupied was lightly wooded and covered with rocks and big boulders. The men took what protection they could behind the trees and rocks. Bullets from the approaching Confederates began to whistle through the leaves and ricochet* off the rocks. They heard a high-pitched screaming noise - the famous Rebel Yell! A very frightening sound. Then they were able to see some of the rebel soldiers coming toward them. Chamberlain commanded "Come to the ready. Take good aim. Fire at will!"

The men fired at the enemy soldiers. The Confederates fired back. Soon the smoke from their muskets almost hid everything from sight. One of the 20th Maine officers told Chamberlain that something strange was going on in their front. He climbed up on a big boulder and peered through the smoke. What he saw gave him a chill. A big enemy regiment was going around their left to hit them from the flank!

In their line of battle the 20th Maine companies stood like this with Company F carrying the flag:

LEFT FLANK	FLAG	RIGHT FLANK
G C H A	F	D K I E

Chamberlain called the company commanders together and told them to go into a new formation that would look like this:

The Road to Little Round Top

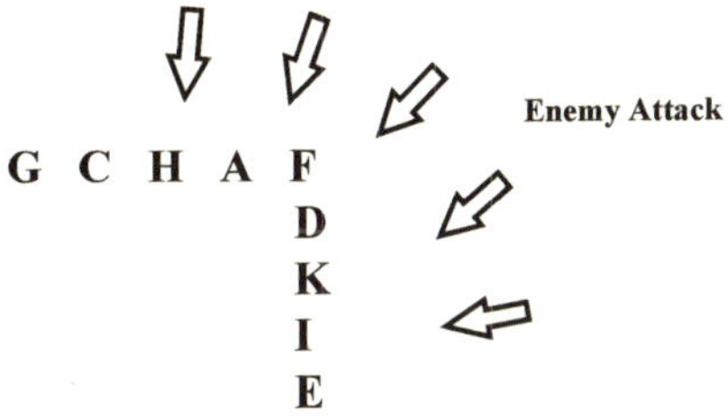

How the regiment moved into this new formation under fire and in the smoke and noise, no one ever understood. But they did it, thanks again to their training. When the big enemy regiment (the 15th Alabama) got around to the 20th's left they thought they would have it "flanked."* But to the Southerners' surprise they met a wall of Yankees and a blast of fire from companies.

The fight continued for more than an hour. The enemy surged forward again and again. Often the combat was hand to hand. The 20th held it's position but lost many men. Also it was running out of ammunition. Chamberlain saw the Confederates preparing for another assault. He could not retreat. His orders were to hold on at all costs. And he could not withstand another attack. What would he do? Perhaps he remembered his father calling to him "Do it! That's how!"

The Road to Little Round Top

Chamberlain stepped to the flag. He shouted Bayonet!"* The men knew what that meant. It meant "Charge!" Up and down the line he heard the clinking of bayonets being fixed to rifle barrels. The men began to shout. Then they jumped up and ran toward the enemy. The left wing that had been bent back swung around abreast of the right. The regiment swept forward swinging like a big gate on a post.

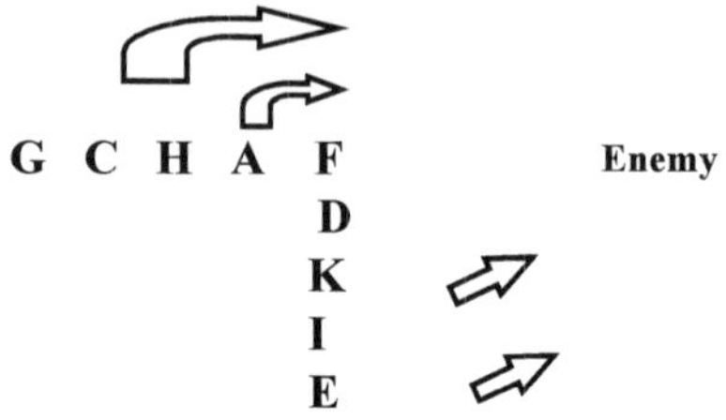

The men of the 20th Maine did not know it when they charged, but the 15th Alabama was not in good shape. Like the Maine men, they had marched most of the night. To reach Little Round Top they had to climb over Big Round Top, because there were Union sharpshooters up there whom they had to clear out. Their water carriers had been captured, so they were very thirsty as well as exhausted.

The Confederates saw the Maine men coming down the hill at them with bayonets. Now let's turn to Company B which had gone into the woods alone. They were cut off by the Confederate advance. They had hidden themselves behind a stone wall. But when they heard the 20th charging they rose up and fired a volley* into the rear of the 15th Alabama.

Some of the Confederate soldiers ran and some surrendered. The 20th Maine kept going and swept the enemy away. They took more than 300 prisoners. But the victory was won at great cost. They had started the battle with 358 men. Now they were down to about 228. They had lost 92 wounded and 38 killed or mortally wounded. Union and Confederate dead and wounded were scattered everywhere.

Chamberlain had a sore foot and he wondered why he was limping. He looked down and saw that his boot had been cut by a bullet. He also saw that the scabbard* of his sword was bent: it had also been struck. In the excitement of battle he had hardly noticed. You can see the boot that was cut (and later patched) in the Joshua Chamberlain Museum in Brunswick, Maine.

As night came, they found that they had more work to do. Another and larger hill called Big Round Top, was hanging over them. It was occupied by the enemy. If the Confederates kept this high ground it would be dangerous. Headquarters sent word that they wanted this big hill taken. The 20th Maine, what was left of it - was lying on the ground exhausted. But at Chamberlain's call, the men got up and followed him up Big Round Top in the darkness, capturing more prisoners, and making the hill secure.

In 1893 Chamberlain would receive the Congressional Medal of Honor - the nation's highest military award. The citation said it was for "daring heroism and great tenacity in holding his position on Little Round Top against repeated assaults and carrying the advanced position on Great Round Top." The medal he received was of a Civil War design. It was later replaced by the design of the Medal of Honor that is awarded today.

The Road to Little Round Top

Describing the battle in later years, the commander of the 15th Alabama wrote, "There never were harder fighters than the Twentieth Maine men and their gallant colonel. His skill and persistency and the great bravery of his men saved Little Round Top and the Army of the Potomac from defeat." Chamberlain's leadership had helped to win the battle even several days before it took place. Remember the mutineers of the 2nd Maine? They were strong, experienced men and there were 120 of them. If Chamberlain had not persuaded all except six to cease their mutiny and fight with the 20th Maine, the fight at Little Round Top surely would have been lost.

Along with the proud sense of achievement there was great sadness in the 20th Maine. They had lost 130 friends and comrades, some killed, some dying in hospitals, some bearing wounds that would hurt them for a lifetime. On July 5 they took up the march in a heavy rain on a road going south with the Army of the Potomac in pursuit of General Lee's Army of Northern Virginia.

At the end of July 1863 army doctors sent Chamberlain home to Brunswick on sick leave. The effects of a sunstroke he had suffered on the march to Gettysburg, the nervous strain of the battle and a malarial fever* had made him ill. Of course Fanny, Grace and Wyllys were delighted to have him home.

When Chamberlain returned to the army near the end of August he found that he had been placed in command of the 3rd Brigade that included the 20th Maine. His brother Tom had been placed in command of the regiment's Company G. For the rest of the year there was a lot of marching as Generals Meade and Lee tried to out-maneuver* one another but no big battles. One freezing night in the middle of November, the men were forced to sleep unsheltered on the ground. Sharing their hardship, Chamberlain slept there too. In the next few days he began to shiver and run a fever. His malarial fever flared up. He was sent to a hospital and again home to Brunswick, where he spent Christmas and New Years with his family. Then he served most of the winter on a court-martial* board in Washington, D.C. He was unhappy there and wanted to get back to the army.

Lincoln was not too happy with General Meade. He had not moved rapidly enough to chase Lee's army after Gettysburg. Meade might have felt that after you've fought a big battle like that, with thousands of men killed and thousands more suffering from wounds, and everyone exhausted, with ammunition and supplies to be replaced, and broken-up units to be reorganized, the army needed some time to recover. Lincoln would have felt that makes no difference - you have to keep after and destroy Lee's army.

Grant Takes Over the Army

Image Courtesy of Patricia Hodgdon

There was a general out West named Ulysses S. Grant. His army had captured Vicksburg, a big Southern city. This victory had opened up the Mississippi River, and he had won some other battles. He always kept after the enemy and never let up. When they asked on what terms they could give up he said "unconditional surrender!"* Lincoln kept Meade in charge of the Army of the Potomac but he put Grant in over-all command of that army and all other United States armies.

Grant had the Army of the Potomac reorganized into three big corps - The Second, Fifth and Sixth. He ordered it to drive south, capture Richmond and destroy Lee's army. Colonel Chamberlain returned to his old regiment for a short while - then he was placed in command of the 1st Brigade, 1st Division, Fifth Corps.

Union Order of Troops

Army
⇩
Corps
⇩
Division
⇩
Brigade
⇩
Regiment

The spring and summer campaign* of 1864 was awful. It was a series of battles - the first in a tangled forest called The Wilderness, which caught fire and burned the wounded lying on the ground. Lee handled his men skillfully. They mostly fought behind entrenchments* and killed more Yankees* than Lee had men in his whole army. But although he never seemed to win a battle, Grant kept his army moving south. He knew that the North had more men, more resources than the South. He would use them to wear Lee out.

The Union army got close to Richmond, but it was too strongly fortified to attack so Grant decided on another strategy.* He would capture Petersburg, a city to the south of Richmond. Through this city ran railroads and other lines of communication that carried most supplies into Richmond. If he could capture Petersburg he could cut off their lines of supply and starve Lee's army out. Capturing Petersburg was a good idea but the Army of the Potomac moved too slowly. By the time it arrived a strong Confederate force had reached there ahead of it. The city was surrounded by fortifications* and entrenchments. They were manned by riflemen and artillerymen with plenty of ammunition.

On June 18, leading his brigade on an attack against one of the enemy's strongest position, Chamberlain was shot. The bullet went through his body from hip to hip. He lay for some time on the ground with shells falling all around him and dust and dirt flying everywhere. Then he was carried to a safer place and finally to a field hospital three miles behind the lines.

Hardtack & Coffee, c. 1887

The 20th Maine had been held in reserve,* so it had not participated in the attack. However, Tom Chamberlain, now a Captain, heard that his brother had been wounded. He searched all over for Joshua and finally located him. He went to the field hospital. With him he had the 20th Maine surgeon, Dr. Abner O. Shaw and another surgeon from the brigade.

Grant Takes Over the Army

When Tom and his doctor friends arrived at the hospital tent the doctor in charge told them that Joshua could not survive. Before it stopped the bullet had cut some blood vessels and fractured bones. "Maybe we can't save him, but let us try," Dr. Shaw said. The two doctors were given permission to operate.

Working at night, Doctor Shaw and the other surgeon cut out dead tissue, tied off several blood vessels, and removed the bullet. Once they stopped operating because they were causing him so much pain. But he asked them to go on - he really wanted to live. And the operation succeeded in saving his life. You can see the bullet Dr. Shaw removed at the Joshua Chamberlain Museum.

When General Grant was notified by General Meade, Commander of the Army of the Potomac, about the charge Chamberlain had led and his wound, he promoted him to a full brigadier general. Then he sent the papers to President Lincoln and the U. S. Senate to be confirmed. Of course, they were confirmed.

On the day after his operation, Chamberlain was in terrible pain and still thought he would die. He wrote a farewell letter to Fanny. You can see it at the Joshua Chamberlain Museum. He was taken to the Naval Hospital in Annapolis, where several skilled physicians attended him and Fanny came to help take care of him. His brother John came from Maine to see him too. By mid-July the danger seemed to be past. By the end of August he was able to sit up a good part of each day. On September 20, 1864, Chamberlain was sent home to Brunswick to spend some time with his family and to get his strength back. Again, Fanny, Wyllys and Grace were overjoyed to have him home. Everyone expected him to stay at home. But Chamberlain was determined to go back and help his comrades. After only a month - although very weak – he returned to the army.

When he returned to the army he found it engaged in siege warfare.* Petersburg was surrounded by a ring of fortifications. The Army of the Potomac was dug in around it in a ring of entrenchments - often not more than a hundred yards away. The opposing forces attacked each other with artillery shells, mortars* (firing high-flying shells that came almost straight down) and constant sniping.

Chamberlain was now a full brigadier general* in command of the Fifth Corps' 1st Division's, First Brigade. Nothing much happened in November. But in December the corps made a raid to the South to destroy the Weldon Railroad which was allowing the besieged Confederates to get supplies by a roundabout route. On the way back Chamberlain was exposed to an ice storm. He began to feel sick and realized that he had returned to the field too soon. Taken to Philadelphia, he was treated by one of the most skillful surgeons in the nation, and his condition greatly improved. Then he was sent back to Brunswick again to rest and get well.

Grant Takes Over the Army

January and February were cold and snowy months in Maine, as they usually are. Chamberlain stayed inside his warm house and slowly gained strength. His mother wrote to him urging him not to go back to the war. He had done and suffered enough she thought. But Chamberlain answered, "I owe the country three years service...and I am not scared or hurt enough yet to be willing to face the rear when other men are marching to the front." So he went back to the army near the end of February.

Toward the end of March General Grant launched a big attack aimed at cutting one of the last lines of supply into Petersburg - the South Side Railroad. If that could be done Petersburg and Richmond would fall. The Fifth Corps was part of this attack and Chamberlain's Brigade led this advance up a road called the Quaker Road. After being driven back about a mile the Confederates re-formed their line behind strong breastworks* on the edge of a wood. The 1st Brigade advance came to a halt. Chamberlain put half of his brigade on the left of the Quaker Road and part on the right, then led a charge straight up the road at the enemy breastworks.* Chamberlain's excited horse got a little too far ahead of the troops. Chamberlain gave him a quick check. The horse reared up and a bullet aimed at Chamberlain went through the big muscles of the horse's neck. The bullet bruised the General's arm, struck a hand mirror in his breast pocket, and followed two of his ribs around and came out the back of his coat.

Knocked unconscious, Chamberlain fell forward and instinctively grasped the horse's neck. The two of them, bleeding together, made such a gory sight that a dispatch went to the editor of a New York newspaper who reported his death. But Chamberlain recovered and so did his horse. It was his special, favorite horse, Charlemagne. As Chamberlain was coming to, the division commander, General Griffin, came up and said "My dear General, you are gone." Griffin meant that he was dying. But Chamberlain misunderstood him. He thought Griffin was referring to the right of his brigade line, which had broken and was retreating.

Straightening up, Chamberlain spurred his wounded horse away from the astonished Griffin. He rode into the midst of his retreating soldiers and rallied them into another attack. This attack was partially successful. It recovered a foothold in the enemy breastworks. A little later in the day, as the fight was still roaring around the breastworks and the outcome was still uncertain, Chamberlain led another attack riding, not Charlemagne, who had lost a lot of blood and could not continue, but a borrowed horse. The Confederate defenders gave way and retreated. Not long afterward Chamberlain would receive another promotion to brevet major general* "for conspicuous gallantry in action on the Quaker Road, March 29, 1865."

Charlemagne recovered from his wound and at the end of the war Joshua Chamberlain purchased him from the government. He was brought to Maine and lived a long, happy life at the Chamberlain summer home where he was buried.

On March 31, 1865 the Confederates launched a heavy attack that drove the Fifth Corps back and regained all the lost ground. The corps was about to be disgraced. Its commander, General Warren came to Chamberlain. He was lying on a pile of straw, suffering from his old wound and his new one. But

Warren asked him to lead a counterattack.* As Chamberlain started to protest, Warren said very grimly "We have come to you: you know what that means." Chamberlain got up and led the attack. He drove the enemy back even beyond the line they started from.

The final battle of the Petersburg campaign was at a place called Five Forks. The Confederates were entrenched with their main line of defense along the White Oak Road. It was on April Fool's Day, 1865 and the Fifth Corps got fooled. It had been given a bad map and missed the entrenchment entirely: going right by the end of it. Chamberlain helped get it turned around and they attacked the Confederates from the rear. Chamberlain was very active in the battle of Five Forks. He dashed around rallying the men. He herded the men in the right direction, and pressed the attack. General Sheridan, the cavalry* commander in command of the whole campaign came by and yelled "By God, that's what I want to see! General officers at the front:"

Five Forks was a great victory for the Union. Thousands of Confederate soldiers were captured. The Fifth Corps was able to cut across the South Side Railroad. Chamberlain's brigade captured the last Confederate train that tried to make a run out of Petersburg. Word came that Petersburg had fallen, the Confederate government in Richmond was breaking up. Lee's army was retreating to the south.

General Lee was hoping that he could get far enough south so that he could link up with other Confederate forces and continue the war. The Army of the Potomac set out in pursuit. Its soldiers had been on many hard marches before but never on one like this. On April 4 the Fifth Corps moved more than thirty miles. The next week there was some fighting with the rear guard* of Lee's army, but for Chamberlain's Brigade in the Fifth Corps it was mostly marching. They were hurrying to get ahead of the Confederates and cut them off. On April 8 orders came to march all of the following night. They marched 29 miles before they had to drop exhausted beside the road and sleep.

Honor Answering Honor

In the night a cavalryman came dashing up the road. He delivered a message to Chamberlain. It was from General Sheridan, the cavalry commander, to all infantry commanders. It said "I have cut across the enemy at Appomattox Station.... if you can possibly get your infantry up here tonight, we will have great results in the morning." Chamberlain's men, had nothing to eat for hours and only a moment's sleep. They were still cold and sore-footed. But at the command "Forward," then got up and marched on!

By the time the sun came up on April 9th Chamberlain and his men, along with other troops of the Fifth and another corps had won the race. They had joined Sheridan's cavalry to cut off the Confederate's retreat. And the Sixth and Second Corps were attacking Lee from behind. He was in a trap. His men were famished and weak, his supplies and ammunition almost gone. Firing broke out. There was fighting for a while. Chamberlain saw one of his young officers killed by a shell. Then he saw a young Confederate officer riding toward them on his horse waving a white towel. The towel was a sign of truce.* The young officer got off his horse and said "Sir, I am from General Gordon. General Lee desires a cessation of hostilities until he can hear from General Grant as to the proposed surrender."

Still, Chamberlain did not know what was happening. He received orders to halt and cease firing. He heard that there was a truce on until one o'clock. One o'clock came and nothing happened. Chamberlain was preparing to make or receive an attack when suddenly he saw a horseman pass by. It was Robert E. Lee in a splendid uniform. Shortly afterward General Grant rode past. Chamberlain later described him as being very plainly dressed. "Slouched hat without cord, common soldier's blouse, unbuttoned, on which however, the three stars; high boots, mud-splashed to the top; trousers tucked inside..." General Grant was going to meet Lee at a house in a place called Appomattox Court House. There they would agree and sign the documents on the terms of surrender.

McLean House at Appomattox Court House where surrender took place.

When the soldiers knew it was all over they went wild. Caps, muskets, knapsacks, canteens, and other articles went flying into the air. Men laughed, shouted, shook hands, hugged each other and even cried. Realizing that this was a historic event, everyone tried to get a souvenir. An apple tree that Robert E. Lee had sat under to rest for a while was cut down and cut up into fragments. The whole tree disappeared. Even the roots were cut up into pieces for souvenirs.

The Union army shared its rations with the starving Confederates. That night the two armies rested side by side without fear. Their picket lines* were within speaking distance of one another. They talked back and forth. A Fifth Corps soldier said of the Confederates "They, like ourselves were glad the war was over." The Confederates wanted simply to go home. But Grant thought there should be a formal ceremony. The Confederates should lay down their arms and flags. General Chamberlain was told by his division commander that he was to receive the arms and flags of the Confederate infantry. "Grant wants them treated with respect," he was told. Chamberlain thought "I'll do more than that. I'll have our troops stand at 'shoulder arms'* in recognition." But he knew this would get him into trouble.

Honor Answering Honor

Chamberlain knew that many people up North who had lost sons, husbands, brothers and friends to Confederate bullets and shell, were angry at the South. And many in Congress wanted to punish the Confederates.

General John B. Gordon, C.S.A.
Photo Courtesy of Library of Congress

General Gordon led the surrendering troops. He rode at the head of the column of troops. His head was bowed. He looked sad and depressed. But when he heard the sound of shifting arms, he looked up. He realized his troops were being recognized and welcomed back into the Union. He wheeled around and gave a command for his men to pass at the position of "carry arms."* This meant they were returning the gesture. This gesture by General Chamberlain, soldier to soldier, was a recognition of respect for the men they fought. He called it, "Honor answering honor."

Carry Arms

As each Confederate division came abreast of Chamberlain's troops, it halted The men faced toward them. The officers made sure they were all in line. Then, as Chamberlain described it "They fix bayonets, stack arms; then, hesitatingly, remove cartridge boxes and lay them down.....lastly, they tenderly fold their flags, battle-worn and torn,.......and lay them down...."

And only the Flag of the Union greets the sky!"

Civilian Life Again

Only three days after the surrender, news arrived that President Lincoln had been assassinated. The joy of victory turned to shock and sorrow. It was one of many sorrows. In the North and South families were grieving for the deaths of half a million men and even more had been wounded or sickened by disease. In the South, homes and factories lay in ruin. The railroads had been destroyed. The people were poverty stricken. The war had been a great tragedy. Although the nation had been reunited and the slaves had been freed, their race in America still had a long way to go before becoming free and equal.

Joshua and Tom Chamberlain returned to Maine as war heroes. Joshua had commanded troops in 24 battles. He had been struck by shot or shell six times. Tom also had been wounded and had risen from the rank of private to lieutenant colonel. Joshua had risen from lieutenant colonel to brevet major general.* He was commanding a division at the war's end. Joshua was asked to run for Governor of Maine on the Republican ticket. He won by one of the largest majorities ever recorded in the state. He served four one-year terms as governor of Maine.

One of Chamberlain's worries as governor was that too many young people were leaving the state. He worked to attract new industries to Maine so they could find jobs here. He promoted a plan that brought a large group of people from Sweden to settle in Northern Maine. They formed the towns of New Sweden, Stockholm and other communities and added many valuable citizens to the population. Of course, like all governors, Chamberlain had many problems. The Republican party leaders, like all party leaders, wanted him to do the things that they thought would get votes. In that way they could continue to keep one of their party in office.

Civilian Life Again

But Chamberlain always insisted on doing what he thought was right. That sometimes made trouble for him.

At the end of his last term as governor, Chamberlain was asked by Bowdoin College to become its president. He accepted. In 1871 Bowdoin was not the college it is today. Its enrollment was low. Its funds were low. And its program of studies was behind the times.

In Chamberlain's inaugural address he told the faculty, trustees and overseers that there ought to be improvements. The world was rapidly changing. There ought to be more courses in the sciences. Women ought to be admitted. (Bowdoin was then an all-male college.) Chamberlain introduced some of these changes. But at that time, the college did not have the money to continue them. It was not until some years afterward, after Chamberlain's presidency, that the fine programs he envisioned came into being.

After the fighting had ended, many people thought there would be no more wars. The Civil War had been too awful. People would have more sense than to start another one. Chamberlain did not agree. He believed there would be more wars and he thought of the thousands of soldiers in the Civil War who had lost their lives because of poor care and leadership.

Chamberlain introduced a program to train them. It was quite popular at first. The students enjoyed marching and drilling with the guns. But they grew more and more tired of it. Finally they said "No more! We won't do it anymore." It was mutiny! Chamberlain sent all the mutineers home. He sent a letter to their parents. The letter said they could only come back if they signed a statement agreeing to obey the rules of the college. All but three came back. But the military program declined and was finally shut down.

During his busy life at Bowdoin, Chamberlain found a few hours for fun and recreation. In 1871 he bought a 26-foot sloop that he named Wildflower. In it he sometimes went sailing with Fanny, Wyllys, Grace and friends over the waters of beautiful Casco Bay.

The Chamberlain Family Sailing
Image Courtesy of Pejepscot Historical Soc.

In 1871 he did something remarkable to his living quarters. Before the war he had lived in a little house on Potter Street in Brunswick. He moved this house to the corner of Potter and Maine Streets in 1867. In 1871 he raised the little house up and built an entirely new first story under it. This is now the Joshua L. Chamberlain Museum.

Something very pleasant happened in 1878. Chamberlain was appointed as United States Commissioner of Education, to represent the U. S. at the Paris Universal Exposition. It was like a World's Fair. He was able to take his whole family and they had a wonderful time in Paris.

In January 1880 there was big trouble in Maine's capital, Augusta. An election for governor, legislators and other officers had taken place in September, 1879. But the results were disputed and the two sides got into a fight. On one side stood the Republicans - on the other, a combination of Democrats and the Greenback Party.* They took up arms and it looked as though there would be a civil war in Maine. The Governor of Maine asked Chamberlain to take command of the state militia to keep the peace. Chamberlain knew he would be getting into a terrible mess but he said "I can't bear to see our fair and orderly state plunged into the horror of a war."

He went to Augusta on January 2, 1880. On January 5 the terms of the existing governor and other officers ended, and a new government had not been agreed upon. That meant that Chamberlain was the only government left! Both sides tried to get him to say that they were the ones that should take office. Both sides offered to back him for U. S. Senator if he would choose them. Chamberlain said no, the Maine Supreme Court should decide. That made both of the contending parties angry at him.

There were plots to get rid of Chamberlain by kidnapping him. These were discovered and prevented. One day an armed mob, threatened to kill him. Chamberlain confronted them and said "I am here to preserve the peace and honor of this state, until the rightful government is seated - whichever it may be, it is not for me to say. But it is for me to see that the laws of this state are put into effect....I am here for that and I shall do it. If anybody wants to kill me for that, here I am! Let him kill!" Then an old veteran of the Civil War burst his way through the crowd and shouted "By God, old General, the first man that dares to lay a hand on you, I'll kill him on the spot!" People in the gathering muttered to one another. Soon the mob melted away. After several days more, the Maine Supreme Court settled the matter. It decided that the Republican candidate for governor had been rightfully elected. Chamberlain had saved Maine from the bloody horror of war. But he had ruined himself politically. Both sides were angry at him because he had not done as they wished. There was no chance now of his ever becoming a senator or holding any important public office.

Meanwhile Chamberlain's old wound – the one he received at Petersburg - was bothering him much of the time. On April 19, 1883, he underwent another major operation in Boston. The surgeon said it was a success but afterwards he felt very weak. He decided to resign as president of Bowdoin and did so that summer.

The Final Years

During the last 17 years of his life, after resigning from the Bowdoin presidency, Chamberlain was engaged in several businesses in the recreational development of Florida and in various industrial enterprises in the North.

In late 1899 Chamberlain's friends tried to get him appointed Collector of Customs at Portland. This was an important and well-paying job that had usually been awarded to ex-governors, ex-senators and the like. But Chamberlain did not have enough political backing to get it. He had to settle for the second-best job, Surveyor of the Port of Portland. Before Chamberlain started on his new job in Portland, he went on a trip to Italy and Egypt. He saw the volcano Vesuvius erupting, several cities in Italy, and all the sights in Egypt - the pyramids, the tombs and temples and the Nile River. Fanny did not go with him. Her eyesight and general health was failing.

In 1905 Fanny fell and broke her hip. In October of that year she died at the age of 80. Her funeral services were conducted in the First Parish Church where she and Joshua had been married on a December day in 1855. She was buried in the family plot in Pine Grove Cemetery. Joshua had engraved on the back of her grave stone the word "Unveiled." What meaning did he intend? That her eyes are now seeing clearly? Nobody knows.

Chamberlain kept the house in Brunswick but mostly for summer use. To save going back and forth and to make his life a little easier, he bought a house on Ocean Avenue in Portland. His son Wyllys lived with him and had a business in Portland not far from the custom house where his father had his office. They could ride to and from work together on the trolley.

One of the pleasures of his life was in visiting his granddaughters. His daughter Grace had married Horace Allen, a well-to-do attorney in Boston. They had three daughters, Eleanor, Beatrice and Rosamond. They lived in a beautiful home in Boston with a summer place in Duxbury, on the coast. Chamberlain went to see them often and sometimes visited him at the house in Brunswick or in Portland.

Rosamond Allen lived to be 101. She died in the year 2000. She always remembered her grandfather's visits, and could never think of him as a war hero but only as a gentle, cheerful and kind person. She believed that he fought only because he felt it was his duty to help save the Union. She and her sisters called him "Gennie" (short for General) Her mother made him popovers for breakfast.

Being Surveyor of the Port of Portland didn't mean that the old general could sit in an office all day. Sometimes he had to visit the docks and ships in cold, windy winter weather. He was a well-known figure, clad in a long black overcoat, walking with a cane but still erect. Until age 85, long after the age when most men retire, he faithfully worked as Surveyor of the Port.

In February 1914, illness, old age and the old wound caught up with Chamberlain and put him in bed. His daughter Grace traveled from Boston to be with him. Dr. Abner O. Shaw, his old army surgeon who had operated on him at Petersburg, was now an eminent physician in Portland and he came to be at his bedside. Joshua Chamberlain died on February 24,1914.

Flags across the state were lowered to half staff. Newspaper headlines mourned the passing of "The Hero of

Little Round Top." There were two funeral services - one in Portland's City Hall, the other in Brunswick's First Parish Church. Then he was laid to rest in the northwest corner of Pine Grove Cemetery beside Fanny. Soldiers from the National Guard fired three volleys over his grave. A bugler blew "Taps" – the Army's final lullaby.

For nearly half a century after his death the name and heroic deeds of Joshua Chamberlain were completely forgotten. People had other things on their minds - World War I, the Great Depression, World War II. Then in 1957 a book that prominently featured Chamberlain's role in the 20th Maine Regiment appeared. It was ***The Twentieth Maine*** by John J. Pullen, published by J. B. Lippincott Company. In 1958 it was published again in ***Readers Digest Condensed Books*** and was widely distributed across the nation. This awakened much interest in the old war hero.

A flood of books, TV programs and a movie featuring Chamberlain followed. A biography entitled ***Soul of the Lion*** by Willard A. Wallace in 1960, and a novel, ***The Killer Angels*** by Michael Shaara in 1974, and another biography called ***In the Hands of Providence*** by Alice Trulock in 1992. A movie ***Gettysburg*** was released in 1994. And many other books have been written, as well. By 1995 there were only two figures in Civil War history better known than Joshua Chamberlain - Ulysses S. Grant and Robert E. Lee. He was not forgotten after all.

The Final Years

Many things have since happened to keep the memory of Joshua Chamberlain alive. The U. S. Army published a field manual that holds him up as one of its great leaders. He is an inspiration to today's armed forces. Thousands of people visit Little Round Top, where he fought, and his grave in Pine Grove Cemetery near Bowdoin College. The citizens of Brunswick have erected a bronze statue of him in front of his old home and near the First Parish Church and Bowdoin College, all important places in the story of his life.

In 1889 on the Gettysburg battlefield, Joshua Chamberlain gave a talk at the dedication of Maine monuments. He said,

"In great deeds something abides.
On great fields something stays.
Forms change and pass; bodies disappear;
but spirits linger."

He meant that when you visit Gettysburg you can still feel the presence of thousands of men who fought and died there to preserve and pass on to us, the country we have today.

He was speaking, of course, of the battlefield. But the words also describe Joshua Chamberlain's life. It is still an example to us. An inspiration. And an encouragement to do the right thing, no matter how hard it seems. Indeed, something abides.

Glimpses of the Old General

Catherine Smith, who was the General's secretary for the last four years of his life was interviewed in the 1970s by Bette Copeland, the first director of the Pejepscot Historical Society. The following are a few comments which she made:

"Across the ceiling he had his Regimental Flag strung across the ceiling. With age and everything it began to fall down, in places sort of sag. The man who took care of the furnace, he and another student, helped him take the flag down. There was a Mrs. Mary Pennell, Miss Fanny Pennell and Miss Edmunds and myself that helped repair that flag and I'm sure there are all sorts of stitches in it. They put it on the living room floor and the General said "Don't step on it."

"He used to send me off on vacations, of course, all my relatives were in New York, that's where I came from and we'd work a while until we got on each other nerves and then he'd say 'I think you want a weekend in New York' and in those days you went on the boat to New York, you know, so, and I'd come back and we would be all fresh and ready to talk about and write about the war."

"He had twinkling blue eyes. No matter how badly he felt those eyes were always snapping right out at you."

"In 1910 I met him in the Brunswick house on Maine Street at the gate. I saw him many mornings as I walked down Maine Street from MereBrook where we lived and he'd be at the gate and we would say 'Good Morning.' and that was the first time that I had ever met the man although I knew he must be somebody quite famous. He had always a lot of people around him especially the Bowdoin College students. He was always laughing and joking with them. Came Commencement time and I believe Bowdoin was going to present Admiral Peary with a degree so the General, as usual, said he was having a lot of guests, even a Lady Somebody from England. I don't recall her name and later on Admiral Peary would come in and pay his respects but he said there was a hitch. He said he had a housekeeper who had to leave town because of a death in the family. He said Miss Edmunds, his nurse, she didn't know what to do because of Commencement time everybody was using up all the help in town so I offered, 'Do you suppose I could help you out?' He said 'Would you?' You know I always thought it was a scheme of his anyway to get me to say so. So I think that was my first memory of Chamberlain."

"I used to at times when he was busy working on his papers go over the Custom House and use the typewriter over there because the one we had at home was awful and he couldn't see getting a new one."

✠

Glossary

An Army consisted of several corps.

Arsenal - A building where rifles, ammunition, cannon and other arms and equipment is stored.

Artillery - Large weapons, on wheels, firing shells long distances.

Battery - A unit of four or more artillery guns with men who loaded and fired them, plus the horses that drew them and their ammunition from place to place.

Bayonet - A sharp pointed weapon that can be removed from the scabbard and attached to the end of the rifle by the command, "Fix Bayonets!" or simply "Bayonets."

Breastworks - May be earth thrown up from digging an **entrenchment** (see in Glossary), piled up logs or sandbags or other materials to protect against enemy bullets and shells.

Brevet Major General - Brevet was partially an honorary word. A brevet major general received the rank of a major general but did not receive the pay for that rank.

Brigade consisted of several regiments, usually four when the regiments were at full strength.

Brigadier General usually commanded a brigade.

Campaign - A series of battles all for one purpose.

Glossary

Captain - Usually commanded a company, assisted by lieutenants, sergeants and corporals.

Carry arms - A salute made by marching troops.

Cavalry - Cavalry is soldiers mounted on horses. Cavalry could move much more rapidly than infantry (the foot soldiers) but could not usually form so strong a line of battle.

Colonel usually commanded a regiment.

Column – A formation of men for marching – usually four abreast or "a column of fours." This made a tight group that took up as little space as possible on the roads.

Commencement – Graduation ceremony at a college or university in which diplomas are issued.

Commission - A paper giving an individual the authority to act as an officer to be obeyed by the troops under him. Volunteer officers were usually given commissions by the governors of states, regular officers by the President. Commissioned officers were the generals, colonels, lieutenant colonels, majors, captains and lieutenants. Non-commissioned officers were sergeants and corporals.

Company started out to be about 100 men. Companies were not numbered but lettered from A to M. There was no company J because it could be mistaken for "I" in handwriting.

Glossary

Confederacy or **Confederate States of America** - The nation formed by the secession of the states.

Confederate - A citizen or soldier of the Confederacy.

Corps - A unit usually made up of three divisions.

Counterattack – An attack, often unexpected, coming against an advance in progress.

Court Martial - A trial by military officers for crimes or misdemeanors committed in military service.

Division - A unit of three brigades if it was at full strength.

Double-quick - A march that was twice as fast as the normal marching pace.

Entrenchments - Holes or trenches dug into the ground to get into for protection. The dirt from the digging was placed toward the enemy and reinforced with logs or other solid material to form a breastwork.

Flank is the end of a line of battle. To "flank" the enemy meant for one line of battle to get crosswise and at the end of an enemy line of battle. If you were flanked, the enemy could fire lengthwise down your line, like firing down a sidewalk full of people, and if an enemy bullet missed one person it would hit another. Being flanked was what Civil War commanders dreaded most of all.

Glossary

Fortifications - Structures built mostly above the ground for protection.

Greenback Party - A political party that believed our paper money does not need to be backed up by gold or silver, but only a promise to pay by the government. It did not last long.

Infantry - Soldiers who moved and fought on foot with rifles and bayonets.

Lieutenant-Colonel usually was second in command of a regiment.

Line of Battle - When a column went into line of battle facing the enemy it had to stretch out into an extended line, usually two men deep. There were several commands for, and ways of going from column to line of battle, and the men had to be well trained or they would get all mixed up. With regiments and brigades next to one another, a line of battle could be miles in length.

Major General usually commanded an army or a corps. In both armies, the commander of a division was supposed to be a major general.

Malarial Fever - Fever caused by malaria which is an infectious and recurring disease transmitted by mosquitos and characterized by fever and chills.

Maltese Cross - The Army of the Potomac had a system of

symbols that identified quickly any corps, division or brigade. The Corps members had badges marked by a symbol. The Fifth Corps badge was marked with a Maltese Cross. The colors red, white and blue were used to denote 1st, 2nd and 3rd divisions. A square flag meant a division, a triangular flag a brigade. Thus, if you saw a group of soldiers following a triangular flag with a blue border and a red Maltese Cross in the center, you knew instantly that this was the Third Brigade of the 1st Division of the Fifth Corps.

Maneuver - To move in such a way that your soldiers are in a good position to harm the enemy.

Mortars - Huge weapons that looked like cannon but had no wheels. Mortars sat solidly on the ground and pointed at the sky. When fired its shell went up and came almost straight down.

Musket or Rifle - The infantry weapon that soldiers carried. Unlike the modern rifle, it had to be loaded by ramming a bullet and gunpowder into the muzzle end with a ramrod. Loading and firing the rifle took nine different motions and men had to be carefully trained so they would do this by habit, even in the excitement and fear of battle.

Musketry - The fire coming from muskets (rifles.) In the Civil War long lines of soldiers stood up and fired at each other sometimes from distances of 100 yards or less.

Mutiny - Refusal by a group of military service personnel to obey a lawful order.

Muzzle - Forward end of rifle barrel.

Picket line - A thin line of soldiers placed at some distance from an army or other large body of troops to guard against surprise by giving an alarm - usually by firing and retreating to the main body.

Plantation - A large farm operated for profit with slaves doing the work.

Private - The rank of the common soldier, whose main duty was to carry and fight with a rifle.

Quarantine - When there is a contagious disease present the infected people are kept away from others to prevent spread of the disease.

Rear guard - When a large body of troops was moving, a smaller body known as the rear guard often marched some distance behind in order to guard against a surprise attack.

Rebellion - Another name for the secession and the Civil War - sometimes called The War of the Rebellion.

Regiment started out to be a group of 1000 soldiers but sickness, wounds and deaths nearly always reduced it to some smaller number. A volunteer regiment was usually called by a number and the name of the state it came from.

Reserve - When entering a battle, a commander often holds some of his troops back. If the enemy breaks through his front line the attack can be met by another line called the reserve.

Glossary

Review - A military ceremony in which a large body of troops is lined up and their commanders and other important officials pass in front of them on foot or on horses. Another way reviews happened was to have officers, etc., standing on a platform while the troops march past.

Ricochet - The sound and spinning action a lead bullet makes as it strikes and bounces off a hard object.

Scabbard - A sheath, attached to an officer's belt, in which he carried a sword or bayonet.

Secede - means "to leave" and it has a special meaning in the Civil War because in 1860 eleven of the states seceded and formed a separate nation.

Sergeant – A non-commissioned officer responsible for supervising groups of men smaller than a company. Sergeants have rank above corporals and privates, and are place in charge due to experience and knowledge of military matters.

Shells - A type of ammunition for artillery. When fired into the enemy some shells exploded and threw fragments of metal to wound or kill. Some shells were just solid metal balls. And some were filled with smaller balls that flew out like a hail of bullets when the shell exploded.

Shoulder arms - Position calling for silence and attention.

Siege Warfare - Usually a long-continued action in which a city and its defenders are completely encircled and cut off from their supplies.

Glossary

Strategy - A general military plan.

Truce - A temporary peace arranged between enemies.

Vaccination - An injection, innoculation or "shot" to prevent disease.

"Unconditional Surrender" - To give up with no promises, no questions asked.

Yankee - What Southern people used to call Northern people - and still sometimes do.